DICE & CARD GAMES

JON TREMAINE

Colour Library Books

THE AUTHOR

Jon Tremaine has been a world-class professional magician and party entertainer for nearly thirty years. He is a member of London's Inner Magic Circle, and has been honoured by them with a Gold Star, the highest award that a magician can receive. He has appeared on television, and has travelled the world entertaining in top night clubs, hotels and cruise liners. His particular speciality is close-up magic, the most difficult branch of magic to perform; its exponents are few, and Jon is undoubtedly one of the best. He is the author of several illustrated books on how to perform magic, and has also written instructional books on two of his other passions: origami and backgammon.

4771
This edition published 1997 by Colour Library Books
© 1996 CLB International, Godalming, Surrey GU7 1XW

ISBN 1-85833-539-6

Credits

Editor
Philip de Ste. Croix

Design and typesetting
Stonecastle Graphics Ltd

Line illustrations
Paul Davies

Production
Ruth Arthur
Neil Randles
Paul Randles
Karen Staff

Production Director
Gerald Hughes

Colour reproduction
HBM Print Singapore

Printed and bound in China
Hung Hing Off-set Printing Co. Ltd

CONTENTS

INTRODUCTION

If you are anything like me, you will by now have had to suffer a decade of computer games. I admit that some of the games are very exciting and that the spectacular graphics used in them are quite amazing. However, they tend to produce legions of alien, zombie-like clones – brainwashed and monosyllabic – unable to live in the real world and totally devoid of social graces. These solitary beings go into a strange, silent decline the moment the screen is switched off! Have you got such a creature living in your house?

I have written this book in the sincere desire that it will help knit your family together again and prove to the aliens (that we laughingly call our children) that we "wrinklies and crumblies" know a thing or two about home entertainment. Our parents taught us! The sight of my mother Betty slowly sliding under the card table, after drinking just one too many G & T's while playing Newmarket, will be a memory that will live with me for ever!

I would like to thank the many friends and relations who have contributed material for this book. Special thanks must go to my wife, Suzy, whose recollections of the games that she played with her sisters and exuberant mother, "Boo" Pasley, have been most instructive and, at times, quite hilarious!

So switch the television off! Delve into this book and teach your children a few of the dynamic, noisy and terribly exciting games that you will find herein. They will thank you for it in times to come. So will *their* children!

The Card Race

Here is a very simple game to start the book. It is easy enough for even young children to be able to play, while the "racing" element means that it can get very exciting as the finishing post comes into view!

Requirements: A pack of cards (excluding the Jokers). A token for each player. These can be numbered discs, coloured counters, chess pieces, or any small objects like buttons, tiddlywinks, etc. You can use any small item as a token as long as each player has a *different* one.

You will need to mark out a chart as illustrated below. A roll of cartridge paper or wallpaper will do fine. It should last you for years so the effort will be worth while.

HOW TO PLAY

A dealer is chosen and given the pack. The players now place their tokens on the playing card symbols at the left-hand side of the chart – either on the ♥, the ♠, the ♦ or the ♣. The choice is up to the player. Everyone is trying to select the winning suit.

Once all the tokens have been committed, the dealer thoroughly shuffles the pack, has them cut, and then proceeds to turn the cards face up one at a time. The value of the card is immaterial – we are only interested in the *suit*.

If the first card is a ♥, it is dealt on the first square on the ♥ line. If the second card is also a ♥, it is placed on the second ♥ square. However, if it is a ♣, it is dealt on the first ♣ square, and so on. You continue in this way until one suit line reaches the winning post.

Those with tokens on the winning suit symbol are rewarded with a small cash or confectionery prize. The dealer is now changed and the next bets are placed. Everyone gets a chance to be the dealer and join in the fun of this exciting game.

Hoy

This is an exciting family card game. Members of large families will be pleased to hear that between four and twelve players may play at a time!

Requirements: Two packs of cards (excluding Jokers). If a large group is taking part, the players can all sit facing one another in a circle on the floor.

HOW TO PLAY

A dealer is chosen by whatever method suits you – cutting the cards, the throw of a die, eldest first... you decide! One pack is thoroughly shuffled and then distributed evenly among the other players. If there are four players, they would each get thirteen cards. If there are seven players, they would get seven cards each, the three remaining cards being discarded. Six players would get eight cards with four discards.

When the participating players receive their cards, they place them *face upwards* in a line or lines in front of them. Taking the second pack of cards, the dealer first removes from it the duplicates of any discards that may have resulted from the distribution of the first pack. The balance of the pack is then thoroughly shuffled and cut.

The dealer now starts to turn over the cards of the second pack one at a time, calling out the name of each card as he does so. Whichever player has the duplicate of this card must turn it face downwards.

Play proceeds in this way, the players turning over the matching cards as they are called out by the dealer. The winner is the first person to turn over all of his or her group of cards. They must shout out "Hoy" to bring their win to the attention of the dealer who rewards them with a small prize.

Play now continues until all the players, bar one, have turned over their cards. A prize is also given to the *last* person to succeed in turning all their cards face down! So there is a prize for the best hand and a prize for the worst!

A new dealer is then selected and the game repeated, as many times as the assembled company wish.

Pairs

Any number of people can play this easy card game, so it is ideal as family entertainment. You have got to have a good memory to succeed – often children prove far superior to adults in this respect, which gives them quite a kick!

Requirements: A regular pack of cards. As long as you have *two* of them, you can keep the Jokers in. For large families the game is best played on the floor with everybody sitting in a circle.

HOW TO PLAY

The pack is thoroughly shuffled. The dealer spreads the cards face downwards all over the playing surface. Each card is separated from its neighbour so that none are touching. Play starts with the person on the dealer's left who turns one card face up, and then another one. If they are *not* a pair, the two cards are turned face down again and the turn passes to the next person on the player's left. He turns over two cards, one at a time. If, by any lucky chance, the two revealed cards constitute a pair, two Aces, two 3s, two Kings, etc., the player wins the two cards as a "trick". He then gets to turn over two more cards. If they are a pair, he keeps these too and goes again. If not, the cards are turned face down again in their original places and the turn passes to the next player.

Play continues until all the cards have been paired off. The player who has collected the most pairs wins the game.

WINNING STRATEGY

This is a memory game. That is why you turn over your two cards *one at a time.* If the first card that you turn over is an 8, and someone has previously turned over an 8 without being able to pair it, you will now be able to turn up that 8 as your second card and win a trick – provided of course that you can remember which face-down card it is! This game is a terrific memory exercise and the more you play it, the better your memory will become. At least, that's the theory!

Hidden Treasure

This is a lovely game for you to play with young children. Even four- and five-year-olds can manage it and they join in with great enthusiasm. It is a game that combines memory and luck, and is not as demanding mentally as "Pairs" described opposite.

Requirements: The four Aces and fifteen other cards of any denomination. You will also need a few prizes, like wrapped sweets or small toys.

HOW TO PLAY

Sit the children in a circle on the floor facing inwards. Show them the nineteen cards and point out that there are only four Aces (of course) and these are the Treasure Cards!

Mix all the cards together so that nobody knows their order. The treasure is well and truly hidden. Spread them out in the middle of the circle, face downwards.

Each child in turn is asked to turn over *one* card. If it is an Ace, they win a prize. If the card is not an Ace, they do not win and that card has to to be turned face downwards again. The Aces are left face upwards as and when they are found. Play proceeds in a clockwise direction.

It is amazing how quickly the children learn to remember where the wrong cards are – the ones that have previously been shown not to be Aces – so that they don't make the same mistakes as the other players.

You will usually be able to complete at least two circuits, but if all the Aces are found before a circuit is completed, gather in all the cards, give them a good shuffle and lay them out on the floor again. You re-start the game from the point that you left off, thus ensuring that everybody has equal turns.

Newmarket

This was my mother's favourite card game and she was real "wiz" at it! It is a simple game to learn and its strategy should be well within the grasp of most people. Newmarket has many disguises – it is also known as Michigan, Chicago, Saratoga, Boodle, and Stops. The rules vary, but this is the version that I enjoy most. It is usually played for small stakes – money or sweets!

Requirements: A full deck of 52 cards. The A♥, K♣, Q♦, J♠ from another pack.

These four cards are placed at the centre of the table in a face-up row and are known as "the Boodle".

HOW TO PLAY

Any number of players from three to eight may join in. The cards are cut to decide a playing and seating order. Aces count *high* in Newmarket. The deal rotates clockwise around the group for each round during the course of the game. The object of the game is to get rid of all your cards and, in the process, collect money (or whatever stakes you are playing for) along the way! Before the cards are dealt out, all players must put one unit stake on each of the four Boodle cards. The dealer must put *two* on each.

The deck is now shuffled and dealt out completely. An extra hand is dealt to the left of the dealer. This is called "the Widow". Because all the cards are dealt out, some players may get one card more than the others. That's life!

If the dealer is unhappy with the hand that he has dealt himself, he may exchange it for the Widow hand. He is not allowed to look at the cards in the Widow before the exchange is made, however, and his original hand must be placed face downwards on the table unseen by the other players.

If the dealer decides *not* to take the Widow, he may auction if off to the other players. The highest bidder pays the dealer the agreed amount. If it is not purchased or used by the dealer, it just stays put as a "boggy" hand.

Play starts with the person on the dealer's left. He may select any suit and must lead with the *lowest* card that he possesses in that suit. He lays it face up on the table just in front of himself, and calls out the name of this card (e.g. 2 ♦). The player who holds the next card of the same suit in ascending order (3 ♦) now plays it. Play continues like this, jumping from one player to another, in haphazard order, as the cards dictate. If you are fortunate enough to have a run of the suit (e.g. 7 ♦, 8 ♦, 9 ♦), you should get rid of all the cards in the run at the same time.

Play in that suit will obviously eventually come to a halt, either because someone plays the A ♦ or one of the hidden cards in the Widow prevents further progress. The person who played the last card now lays from a different suit, starting of course with the lowest card that he holds in that suit. If he only holds cards of the suit that has just been "stopped", he must pass and the person on his left takes up the play.

A player's discards must be played face upwards in a pile directly in front of him and must not be spread out so that he could look back at previously played cards.

The first player to get rid of all the cards in his hand wins the round and the other players pay him *one unit for each card that they still hold in their hands!*

THE BOODLE

If, in the course of play, you lay down a card that matches one of the Boodle cards you win all the money that sits on it! If the money resting on a Boodle card is not claimed during a round, the stakes remain on it as a ride-over into the next round when the players again place one unit on each of the four Boodle cards, while the dealer puts two units on each. In this way a nice kitty can accumulate on a lucky card.

PENALTY

If a player fails to play a card in sequence that he could have played, he must pay a penalty of one unit to each player. If, by this omission, he prevents someone from claiming a Boodle prize, he must also make good this loss to the player in question. The money that lies on the Boodle card carries over into the next round. It is up to the other players to point out a mistake of this nature; it is not the responsibility of the perpetrator to point it out. So keep your eyes peeled!

WINNING STRATEGY

- The dealer has an obvious advantage because of his access to the Widow hand. If he decides to exchange his original hand for the Widow, he should strive to remember the values of the cards in his original hand, so that he can work out which runs will be blocked by missing cards.
- If you hold a Boodle card, you should lead with the same suit as the Boodle.
- If you hold an above average number of cards of one suit, you should lead with this suit in an attempt to win the round.
- If you hold a hand with an above average number of high cards in it, you should hold onto it even if it does not contain Boodle cards, because the chances of it winning the round for you are high.
- If you still hold low cards in a "stopped" suit, you must get rid of them as quickly as possible.

Cuckoo

The cuckoo is a gluttonous bird that forces its way into another's nest and disrupts the quiet life and habitat of its neighbours. This card game is a bit like that! Up to twenty can play, although it is best enjoyed with six to eight participants.

Requirements: A standard pack of 52 cards. Aces rank *low*. Three chips, coins or matchsticks for each player.

HOW TO PLAY

The object of the game is *not* to get caught with the lowest card.

A dealer is chosen in the normal way and he deals one card to each player. The person on the dealer's left starts. He can do one of two things:

- Call "Stand" and keep his card.
- Call "Change" and exchange his card with that of the player on his left.

So, if player A calls "Change", player B must exchange cards with him *unless* it is a King. He must show the King and this automatically freezes player A who must now "Stand", whether he likes it or not.

Player B can now choose to stand or change. He would be foolish to change in the above example, because a King is the highest ranking card in the game. However, the choice is his. Player C now has the two choices, and so on clockwise around the circle.

Note: If you pass on an Ace, 2 or a 3, you must do it with the card *face up* – thus displaying its value to all the other players. All other cards should be passed on face downwards. When the play gets back to the dealer, he is allowed the same two choices. He may choose to stand. If however, he chooses to change, he has to cut the remainder of the pack and exchange his card for the top card of the cut. The cruel rule in this case is that if he should cut a King, he automatically loses the round! Sad!

Once the dealer is done, the players all reveal their cards and the person holding the lowest card puts a counter into the pot. If there are equal losers, they both have to put into the pot!

The game continues until all but one of the players have lost all their chips. The remaining player claims all the chips in the pot. If six people were playing, that would be 18 chips – a win of 15!

Pontoon

This is a very good family game even though, in its casino guise as Blackjack or Vingt-et-Un, it has acquired gambling overtones. My personal view is that even children should be taught to play *for* something – be it counters, matches, sweets or even buttons. When there is a wager of some sort, it adds a little extra spice to a game and teaches the children the art of losing gracefully. Agree the minimum and maximum stakes allowed before you start to play.

Requirements: A standard pack of 52 cards. Plenty of counters for each player. Three to six people can play.

HOW TO PLAY
Cards are assigned point values as follows:

> Ace = 1 *or* 11, at the discretion of the player
> All court cards (Kings, Queens and Jacks) = 10
> Pip cards (2s to 10s) score their face value

A banker is chosen (the highest card cut gets the honour) and all players compete against the banker. You beat the banker if the total of your hand is better than his, while still totalling 21 or under. During the course of each round you may accept extra cards from the banker to improve the score of your hand. Your objective, therefore, is to score 21, or as near to it as you can get, without "busting". You may use as few as two, and a maximum of no more than five, cards to achieve this. One of the advantages of being banker is that you pay out only on hands that beat your score, not those that equal it. You get nothing for a draw in this game!

After the pack has been thoroughly shuffled and cut, the dealer distributes one card face down to each player including himself. The banker is not allowed to look at his card at this stage. The other players look at their individual cards and bet on them, placing their stakes just in front of their cards, which are replaced face down after they have been inspected.

Once all the bets are in place, the banker deals another face-down card to each player. The banker now completes the play of the first player on his left (as described below), then completes the hand of the second player, and so on, finally turning his own two cards face upwards and completing his own hand. Then he settles bets as applicable.

HOW TO PLAY YOUR HAND

If the two cards that a player receives total 21 (an Ace and a court card or an Ace and a 10), he lays them face up on the table immediately and declares "Pontoon". He will become banker once the present round is completed, provided that none of the other players declares "Pontoon" too. If he declines to accept the bank (it is optional), the player sitting on his left is offered it. If the banker should also declare "Pontoon" when he comes to turn his cards up, he retains the bank and wins all bets because, of course, he only pays out on hands better than his own! And you can't get better than Pontoon. Here are a few examples of Pontoon hands:

If, however, the two cards do not constitute a Pontoon, the player has three options:

- He can *stick*. Provided that his total is not less than 16, he can refuse to take a further card. He stands with what he has got.
- He can *buy* another card for an amount not exceeding his original stake. This card is dealt face down by the banker, so that only the buyer knows its value.
- He can *twist*. This means that he receives a "free" card and this is dealt face up on the table in front of the player.

After a player buys a card (assuming of course that he has not gone bust), all three options are open to him again: he can stick, buy or twist. If a player twists, he may twist again but is not now allowed to buy.

The player will eventually either stick or bust. If he is busted, the banker immediately collects the amount of the bet.

The second player is now serviced by the banker, and so the sequence continues around the table until everyone has either stuck or gone bust. Lastly the banker turns up his own hand and moulds it to as near 21 as he dare. He deals more cards face up to himself if he requires them. If he busts, he pays out a stake equal to that bet by all the players who have remained in. Otherwise he stops at a total he thinks acceptable, and only pays players who can beat his figure. The two exceptions to this are **five-card tricks** irrespective of their total, and **Pontoons** – these are both paid double the total stake. Pontoons have already been explained; five-card tricks are hands containing five cards that do not exceed 21 in total – they are quite hard to get.

SPLITS

If a player's first two cards are both of the same value, e.g. two 9s, two Aces etc., he may split them – placing the pair side by side and face up on the table. I stress *"may split"* because it is not compulsory. A bet equal to the original stake is placed on this second card and the banker deals a card face down to each – the player is now actually playing two hands at once. A third, even a fourth duplicate card may be received in this way and also split if desired. So a player could end up playing four hands simultaneously.

The exception to this are Aces. These may only be split once and may only receive one card each. If a Pontoon results on either or both, the payout from the banker is even money not double as is the case on a "pure" Pontoon.

WINNING STRATEGY

- Bet the maximum on an Ace. There are 16 cards in the pack with a value of 10, so your chances of making a Pontoon are pretty good.
- Bet a medium stake on court cards and 10s.
- Bet the minimum on medium value cards.
- Always split Aces and 8s.
- Do not split Kings, Queens, Jacks or 10s because together they already total 20, which is a strong score.
- Do not split 5s. They total 10 which is a good basis on which to receive a third card.
- Do not split 2s and 3s – they could well form the basis of a lucrative five-card trick.
- Buy cards until your hand totals twelve or over – then twist.
- Always take the bank if you have the opportunity to do so.

To give you a clear idea of how Pontoon is played, I shall now take you through a demonstration game. Follow it through from start to finish. We will assume that there are five players: **A**nne, **B**ill, **C**laire, **D**avid and **E**dward. Edward won the cut and became banker. This was the first deal and the number of chips bet:

A	B	C	D	E
K♦	A♣	7♠	4♥	?

Units bet:

| 2 | 3 | 1 | 1 | |

This was the second deal:

| 10♥ | 6♦ | 8♥ | 4♦ | ? |

Anne with a total of 20, sticks: K♦ 10♥

Bill with 7 or 17 buys 3 cards for 1 unit each. He gets a five-card trick for a total outlay of 6 units: A♣ 6♦ 2♠ 4♣ 7♥

Claire with an awkward 15 twists – and busts: 7♠ 8♥ Q♥

David with a pair decides to split. His first hand busts after he twists: 4♥ J♦ 9♣. He buys a card for his second hand for 1 unit and finishes with a healthy 21: 4♦ 7♣ Q♠

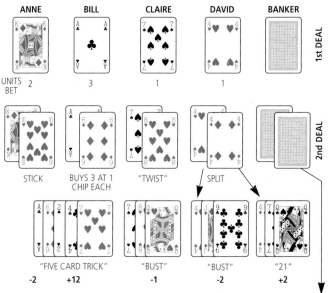

ANNE	BILL	CLAIRE	DAVID	BANKER	
UNITS 2 BET	3	1	1		1st DEAL
STICK	BUYS 3 AT 1 CHIP EACH	"TWIST"	SPLIT		2nd DEAL
"FIVE CARD TRICK"		"BUST"	"BUST"	"21"	
-2	+12	-1	-2	+2	

Edward (the banker) now discloses a hand of 20 and pays out on 21s, Pontoons and five-card tricks: 10♥ Q♦.

After settling the bets the account stands as follows:
Anne -2
Bill +12 (five-card tricks pay double)
Claire -1
David 0
Edward -9

BANKER PAYS 21s, PONTOONS AND 5-CARD TRICKS

Bingo!

Have you got an old pack of cards in the house? If you have, you will easily be able to make up the eight plaques needed for this game. Once made, the plaques will last you for years and give hours of fun.

Requirements: A pack of cards minus the four Jacks. A pencil and paper for scoring. An old pack of cards, also minus the Jacks.

Stick the old playing cards onto cardboard backing so that you end up with eight plaques as shown in diagrams A-H. Follow our illustrated layouts carefully and exactly. If old cards are not available, you could depict the appropriate cards in a very simple way, like this:

HOW TO PLAY

Up to eight players can participate in this game. A dealer is chosen. He first thoroughly mixes the plaques and each player chooses one at random. This is their "Bingo" card! If less than eight players participate, the surplus plaques are evenly distributed among the players if numbers allow. They then play *two* plaques at the same time. Any plaques that are still surplus are put aside. The players set their plaques face up on the table in front of them.

The dealer shuffles the pack of cards and, after it has been cut, starts turning the cards over one at a time, naming the cards as he does so. The player who has the same card represented on his plaque claims the card. He takes it from the dealer and places it alongside its "double" on the plaque. If a card is called that features on a plaque that is not in play, it is placed to one side.

- The winner is the first player to reach a points total of 20, and the scoring is as follows:
- The first player to receive two cards of the *same suit* scores 2 points.
- The first player to receive at least one card of *each suit* scores 3 points.

- The first player to receive four cards of the *same colour* (red or black) scores 4 points.
- The first player to receive *all six cards* on a plaque scores 6 points and calls "Bingo".
- All scores must be on one plaque and not a combination of two.

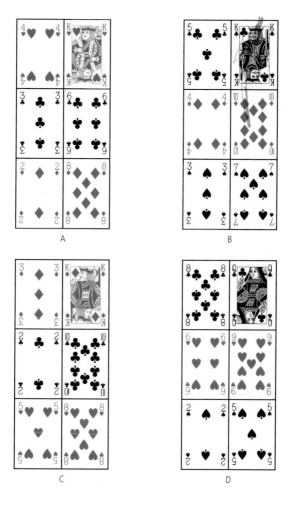

A

B

C

D

E

F

G

H

Once "Bingo" has been called, all the cards are collected, re-shuffled and cut. The next dealer now calls the cards for the next hand. Scores for this hand are added to the scores from the previous hand until one of the players reaches 20. This person wins the game.

Black Lady Hearts

Many variations of the game Hearts exist. This is my personal favourite and I pass it on to you in the confident knowledge that it will soon become a favourite of yours too. I learnt to play Black Lady while still at school. Not being one for energetic ball games, you could usually find me playing Black Lady behind the cricket pavilion – unless my "look-out" saw you coming first!

Requirements: A normal pack of 52 cards. Three to five players can join in – although four is the ideal number.

HOW TO PLAY

The object of the game is to *lose* tricks – especially if the trick contains cards of the Heart suit. Even worse is winning a trick that contains the dreaded Black Lady, the Q♠!

Cards are scored *against* you as follows: each Heart that you win counts 1 point. The Queen of Spades counts 13 points! There is a perverse variation to this rule, called "slamming" or "going for the moon"! That means *winning* all the tricks that contain Hearts *and* capturing the Q♠ trick too! If you can pull that one off, you are allowed to deduct 26 points from your accumulated total. A rare occurrence!

If three people are playing you discard the lowest rated card – the 2♦. The players are now dealt 17 cards each. Four players receive 13 cards from the complete deck. With five players you remove the 2♦ and the 2♣ and each player now gets 10 cards each.

I will now describe the four-handed game. First you cut for dealer – Aces are high in this case. A♠ beats A♥, A♥ beats A♣, A♣ beats A♦. After the deal the players sort out their hands and choose three cards that they do not want. These are slid across the table to the person on your left who must accept them. You accept the three cards that come to you from the player on your right. You must not look at these before you discard your own three cards. On subsequent deals the direction of this exchange is alternated – first left, then right and then (in the four-handed game only) with the player opposite.

Play begins with the holder of the 2♦ (the 3♦ in the case of the three- and five-handed games – the 2♦ having been discarded). Remembering that the object of the game is to lose as many tricks as possible, the player to his left will play his lowest Diamond card – he *must* follow suit if he can. If he has no Diamonds, he can play any card except a Heart or the Q♠. This rule is dropped after the first trick – a player then being allowed to discard *any card* if he is unable to follow suit. The trick is always won by the person who played the highest card of the suit that was originally led. The winner of the trick then leads the first card of the next trick and play proceeds in a clockwise direction as usual. If no one is able to follow suit, the person who led will obviously win the trick and must start the next trick by leading again.

Note: No player is allowed to lead a Heart until either a Heart has been played on a different suit in the course of a trick, or the Black Lady has been played.

Players tot up their running total of penalty points at the end of a pre-arranged number of hands and the person with the lowest score becomes the outright winner.

Here are a few typical tricks to show how play develops:

The 2♦ was led and the 9♦, 8♦ and the Q♦ all followed suit. The player who played the Q♦ wins the trick and leads off:

with 3♦. The A♦ is next and will obviously win the trick. The third player has no more Diamonds, so he takes the opportunity of discarding the mighty K♥. The fourth player is pleased to play the K♦ – an ideal opportunity to unload this high card. The player of the A♦ wins the trick and has also captured the K♥ – much to his annoyance.

Hearts can now legally be led so he leads off with the 4♥, guessing that the other three players must have at least one Heart each, so he cannot win this trick. He judged correctly because the 7♥, 8♥ and 5♥ followed. The unfortunate owner of the 8♥ wins a trick that will count four points against him.

Rummy

No book on family card games would be complete without describing rummy. It is played internationally and forms the basis for many other games, such as Canasta and Kaluki, which are variations on the same theme. The basic game that I am about to describe may be played by as few as two players and by a maximum of six.

Requirements: A standard 52-card deck.

HOW TO PLAY

The object of the game is to be first to get rid of all your cards by melding *groups* and *sequences* and thus collecting points or counters from your opponents. If you decide to play for counters, each player should start with 100.

A *group* is a set of three or four cards of the same rank, e.g. all Aces, all 3s, all Kings, etc.

A *sequence* is a run of three or more cards of the same suit in directly ascending order.

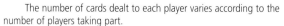

The number of cards dealt to each player varies according to the number of players taking part.

- 2 players get 10 cards each.
- 3 and 4 players get 7 cards each
- 5 and 6 players get 6 cards each.

The cards rate in value from Ace (low) to King (high).

The pack is cut to determine who is to be dealer. The pack is then shuffled and cut and the appropriate number of cards dealt to each player. The balance of the pack is placed face down in the centre of the table and becomes the card *stock*. The top card of the stock is turned face up and placed to the side of the stock pile. It becomes the first card of the *discard* pile.

STOCK PILE   DISCARD PILE

Players sort their cards out into possible scoring groups or sequences so that decision-making as the game unfolds is simplified.

Play begins with the person on the dealer's left and proceeds in a clockwise direction around the group. A player begins by either taking the top card from the stock pile *or* the top card of the discard pile. The aim is to pick up cards that will help make melds (as groups and sequences are collectively known). Any melds that he now has may be laid on the table in front of him face upwards. Once the game is fully in progress, he may also "lay off" cards onto melds that have already been tabled by either himself *or* any other players! Finally he discards one card face up onto the discard pile. This signifies the end of his turn and play passes to the next person on the left.

Note: If a player began his turn by picking up from the *discard* pile, he is not allowed to end the turn by discarding the *same card*.

If the stock pile is exhausted before any player "goes out", the complete discard pile is turned face down to become the new stock pile. The top card is turned face up and placed to the side to form the first card of the new discard pile, just as it was at the start of the game.

It is not compulsory to lay your melds down straight away. Strategically you may not wish to expose your hand just yet. Take care, however, because if another player "goes out", these melds still held in your hand will score against you.

Play continues until one person *"goes out"* by laying down all of his cards. An odd card that cannot be melded may be discarded at this time, but it is not essential to discard a card to "go out" if you can play out all your cards onto the table.

If you manage to "go out" all in one go (without previously having laid down any melds), it is called **"Going Rummy"** and *doubles* the points that you win!

The losing players total up the score of the cards that remain in their hands. Aces count as 1; all court cards count as 10 points each. If you are playing for chips, now is the time to cough up! You must pay the winner 1 chip for each point that you have been caught with. If you are playing for points, the score against each player is recorded – the lowest scorer being the overall winner at the end of play.

WINNING STRATEGY

- Pay particular attention to the way the players on your immediate left and right are playing. You should get some idea of the cards that the person on your right is *not* collecting by watching his discards. It may well be in your interest to go for a meld bearing his preferences and discards in mind. Be careful what you discard to the player on your left. His discards may well help you to work out the melds that he is trying to put together – you must avoid assisting him with favourable discards.
- It is generally good policy to avoid holding on to court cards on the off-chance of using them in a meld. If you have a choice, go for melds that use 2s, 3s, 4s and 5s, because if you are caught with them in your hand at the end of a round, the damage will be less catastrophic.
- Insist that the pack is *thoroughly shuffled* before each round because most of the cards will have been melded into groups and sequences during the course of play and so will not fall randomly and fairly for each player if they are not shuffled adequately.

My Ship Sails

My son, David, has inherited my love of card games. We play at every conceivable opportunity. He is very hard to beat – no matter what the game. I only have myself to blame! We show one another new card games with relish. He taught me this breathtakingly fast game.

Requirements: A standard pack of 52 cards. Four players are the best number for this game, although up to seven can play.

HOW TO PLAY

The object of the game is to be the first to collect seven cards of the *same suit*.

The dealer is chosen by cutting the pack. Aces high! The dealer distributes the cards in a clockwise direction until the players have seven cards each. The balance of the pack is put aside and plays no further part in the proceedings.

Each player sorts his cards out and decides which suit he should collect. This is usually the suit of which he has most cards. A player may decide to "change ships" as play progresses, but always starts out with an objective in mind.

Each player selects one card that he does not want and places it face down on the table in front of him. When everybody has tabled a card, they are slid along to the players on the right. Each player picks up his new card, decides on the next card that he wants to get rid of and places it face down on the table. Once all cards are down, they are passed to the right as before.

The winner is the first person to end up with seven cards all of the same suit. He shouts out "My Ship Sails". If two players go out at the same time, the winner is the first to call. Once people get the hang of this game, it should be played at a furious pace. It is very funny to watch.

A WINNING HAND

Knockout Whist

Many books have been written that deal exclusively with the game of Whist. It would be impossible to do justice to this beautiful and quite complex game in a small book of this type. However, I have included Knockout Whist because it is the simplest of all the Whist derivatives, and will accustom any children playing to the principles of *trick taking* and *trumping*. Up to seven people can play.

Requirements: A standard deck of 52 cards. Aces rank high.

HOW TO PLAY

A dealer is found by cutting for the honour. After shuffling and cutting, seven cards are dealt, one at a time, to each player. The balance of the pack is placed in the centre of the table and the top card turned face up. The *suit* of this card represents *trumps*. It is left face up as a reminder. Trumps are the "master suit"; it outranks the other three suits. Thus, a lowly 2 of the trump suit will beat even a mighty Ace of any of the other suits.

The object is to win all the tricks of a hand. A trick is made up of one card played from each hand, and the winner of the trick is the person playing the highest value card which will either be in the suit that was led by the first player, or a trump. A player must follow suit *whenever possible*. If, however, a player cannot follow suit he may:

- Play a *trump* card. Then the highest trump card played wins the hand.
- Play a card from another suit. This cannot win the trick, so it is effectively a discard.

The winner of the trick *starts off play for the next trick* – leading with a card. The person on his left follows, and so on. When all seven tricks have been played, anyone who has failed to win a trick during that round *drops out of the game*.

The dealer now deals a hand to each of the remaining players. This time they receive *only six cards* each. A new trump suit is selected by turning up the top card of the surplus pile. Once again, any player who does not win a trick in the course of the round has to drop out.

The hands reduce each time by one card, so that if the game reaches the seventh round without someone winning all the tricks in

one hand, the remaining players receive only one card each.
Someone must win now – it's the final showdown in the knockout
competition!

Here are a few sample tricks from a four-handed game:

TRUMPS

FIRST TRICK

SECOND TRICK

Diamonds are trumps. The first player leads with the J♣. This is
followed by the K♣, the 4♣ and the 6♣. The K♣ from player 2
wins the trick. This player starts a new trick by playing 10♥. This is
followed with the 7♥. Player 4 has no hearts so decides to use a
small trump, the 4♦. The last player (player 1) lays the 3♥. So
player 3 wins the trick with his trump. It will be his turn to lead at
trick number three. Get the idea!

Fan Tan

This a very simple and enjoyable family game that up to eight people can play. The rules are straightforward – yet the game requires considerable skill to play well. Fan Tan also goes under the names of Sevens, Parliament and Card Dominoes. This is my favourite card game. I hope that you will come to like it as much as I do.

Requirements: A standard pack of 52 cards. A supply of counters or matches.

HOW TO PLAY

Losses in this game can be quite high, so it is probably not a good idea to play for real money with your family, especially if children are involved. Even so, I still feel that the game is best played for counters, matches or some other form of exchange so that your child can experience the sheer thrill and excitement that this game engenders.

Each player contributes one counter to the pot. A dealer is chosen by cutting the pack. Aces count low. The dealer shuffles and then deals out the complete pack – even if that means that some players get more cards than others. *The players with one card fewer than the others must put an extra counter into the pot.* The players sort their hands into suit and running order.

The person who holds the 7♦ starts the game. He places it face upwards in the middle of the table. Play passes to the person on his left. He has three options:

- Play the next card in sequence either above or below the 7♦ (i.e. the 6♦ or 8♦).
- Play one of the other three 7s and start a new sequence.
- If neither of these two plays is possible, he must put one counter into the pot.

Play now passes clockwise to the next player on the left who has the same three options: laying off onto a tabled sequence, starting a new sequence with a new 7, or chipping in by paying a counter into the pot.

Note: If a player passes when he could play, he is penalized three counters to the pot and five counters each to the holders of the 6 and 8 of the same suit!

Play continues with the sequences extending upwards to the Kings and downwards to the Aces until someone plays his last card. This person wins the pot *plus* one counter for each card held by his opponents. You see now why it is an advantage to have one less card than the other players at the start – an advantage you must pay for!

The next game continues with a dealer and all the players "chipping in" to the pot again. You will understand why I started my explanation by discouraging the use of money when you play this as a *family* game. The pot has the habit of rising very rapidly.

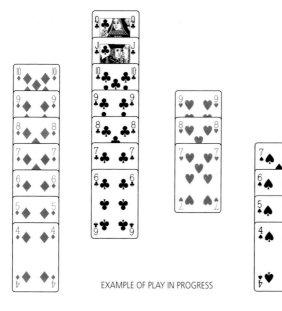

EXAMPLE OF PLAY IN PROGRESS

Cheat

Are you a good liar? Can you look someone in the eye and, with a smile on your face, tell a "pork pie"? If you are good at bluffing, this could well be the game for you! My wife, Suzy, cannot tell a lie and get away with it to save her life – but my son David...! This is a *great* game and particularly suitable for groups that have vastly differing card abilities.

Requirements: Two packs of cards (excluding the Jokers).

HOW TO PLAY

The two packs are thoroughly shuffled together and dealt out one card at a time to each player until the cards have been exhausted. Don't worry if some people get one card more than other players. It is of no importance. The four suits play no part in this game – only the numbers.

The object of the game is to get rid of all your cards.

Play begins with the player on the dealer's left. He removes any card from his hand and places it face down in the centre of the playing area. He names the card. If it was the 6♦ he would say "six". The player to his left now takes a card from his hand, lays it face downwards on top of the first card and calls out "seven". It may or may not be a 7. If it isn't a 7, the player must pretend that it is and try and get away with the "fib"!

The next player lays a card on top of this one and calls out "eight", the next "nine", and so on in an ascending sequence. When the call gets to "King", the next player calls out "Ace", the next "two" etc. Thus the calls continue around the "clock" in a cyclical manner.

Any of the calls may be true or false. The real fun starts when you suspect that a player may be lying. You shout out *"cheat"*! If two people call out "cheat" at the same time, the one who has called first or the loudest becomes the challenger.

The card played must be turned face up for all to see! If it is *not* the card claimed, the player of this card must pick it up again, *together with all the cards beneath it,* and add them to his hand! If, however, it was a truthful call, the challenger has to add all the cards to his own hand! Whatever the outcome of the challenge, the player to the left of the person challenged continues the game and may lay any card he wishes, the previous sequence having been broken.

You are also permitted to cheat by playing *two* cards as if they were only one! Be careful though, because you could well be challenged and have to suffer the consequences! The winner is the person who gets rid of all of their cards first. This is a very difficult thing to do without cheating, so practise your best poker face!

WINNING STRATEGY

- You must practise the art of looking innocent when you are guilty *and* looking guilty when you are innocent.
- Arrange your cards in numerical order so that you can readily see what cards you have got, when the time comes for you to play.
- Try to do your cheating early in the game – before the pile of cards in the centre gets too enormous, and the consequences of being found out correspondingly worse.
- Get rid of the cards that you know you will not be able to play honestly as early as possible.

Donkey

Whether you call this game Donkey, Spoons, Rat-Fink or Pig, makes no difference. Whatever the name, it is still hilarious entertainment for the whole family.

Requirements: A pack of cards. A pencil and paper for scoring. A number of spoons. You will need one spoon less than the number of people playing; i.e., six players need five spoons.

HOW TO PLAY

You do not need all the cards, just "four of a kind" for each player. These can be anything – four Kings, four 3s, four Aces, any four of a kind as long as you have a different set for each player. Any surplus cards are discarded.

Players sit in a circle with the spoons in the centre. It is important that everyone sits the same distance away from the spoons, otherwise someone will have an unfair advantage, when the time comes to make a grab for them. The cards are thoroughly shuffled and then dealt out so that everyone has four mixed cards.

The first objective is to get four of a kind in your hand. You look at your cards and remove the card that you like least and slide it face downwards to the person sitting on your *left*. The person on your *right* has done the same thing and you have to pick up the card that has been slid over to you. This new card may or may not improve your hand. Play continues in this manner until someone gets four of a kind. This player then reaches forward and takes a spoon from the middle. As soon as this happens, *all the other players grab for a spoon.*

Someone will be unlucky and will be out. They are one step towards becoming the "Donkey" and are given the letter **"D"**. The spoons are put back in the centre. The cards are reshuffled and dealt out again and play continues as before until someone else gets four of a kind and reaches for a spoon. Someone will be spoonless again and this person gets a **"D"**. If it was the same player as last time, he gets an **"O"**.

Once a player has collected **D,O,N,K,E** and a **Y**, he is out as far as actually winning the game is concerned. He can still go on playing, however. Play continues until only one person is not a Donkey. This person wins the game, because he has not made a complete *Ass* of himself!

Animal Snap

I had quite a bad stutter as a child, so it is not surprising that I never seemed to win this game! We all know how to play Snap. Animal Snap, however, adds a nice touch of hilarity to this simple family game.

Requirements: A pack of 52 cards. Two packs should be used if there are more than four players.

HOW TO PLAY

Each player adopts the name of an animal. You choose your own name and thereafter are known only by that name. To add some spice to the game, try to use an obscure name like marmoset, or a long name like hippopotamus. Everybody announces the names that they have chosen.

The object of the game is to win all the cards.

The cards are dealt face downwards one at a time until the pack has been evenly distributed among the players. The cards remain in a face-down pile before each player. The dealer calls out "Go". All the players turn their top cards over at the same time and lay them face up in front of their pile. Look at all the face-up cards. If someone has turned over a card of the same value as your own, you must call out *his* animal name as quickly as you can. He will probably have seen your card too and will call out your animal name. The first person to call out the other's name correctly wins all the face-up cards in the two piles. These are added to the bottom of the winner's face-down pile.

If two players call out the animal names *at the same time*, the two piles are combined and left face up in the centre of the table. This pile is called the "Zoo". Cards are now turned up again and if one matches the top card of the centre pile, the person who first calls out "Zoo" wins all the cards. They are placed face down at the bottom of his face-down pile. You can still win cards from your opponents during Zoo time, if other pairs show and you correctly shout out the animal name.

If someone calls you by an incorrect name, they must pay you a penalty of an extra card from their pile for the mistake.

Play continues until someone has won all the cards.

37

Quoits

I was determined not make this book "just like all the others". To this end I have included some of the very *different* games that I have collected on my travels. Quoits certainly comes in that category, yet it is extremely easy to play.

Requirements: Two packs of cards with differently patterned backs (Jokers can be left in). A hat, or a box of about the same size.

HOW TO PLAY

The players are divided into two teams. Each team is given a pack of cards and they distribute them as evenly as possible between all the members of their team. The hat is placed in the centre of the floor. All the players stand around the hat in a circle, holding their cards.

Someone starts by trying to throw one of his cards into the hat. The person on his left now throws a card, and so on. Play continues around the circle until all the cards have been used up. The cards in the hat are now tipped out – sorted into the different back designs – and counted. The team with the most cards in the hat wins. It's as simple as that.

There are a few other rules that apply:
- Five rounds are usually played.
- Cards that come to rest on the rim of the hat do not count, unless any subsequent card knocks it off the rim and into the hat.
- All the players should stand about 2 metres away from the hat. A handicap system could be incorporated – younger people being allowed to stand a little closer.
- There is a definite knack to throwing playing cards. The best way is to hold the card horizontally between your first and second fingers and flick it, as illustrated. In this way, you can get it to fly quite accurately – as always, practice helps.

Crazy Eights

This is another noisy fun game for the whole family. It is called Crazy Eights because the four 8s are "wild" cards which may represent any card you wish. The object of the game is to get rid of all your cards before your opponents do – the eights being of tremendous help to this end.

Requirements: A 52-card pack.

HOW TO PLAY

All the players cut to find a dealer; Aces are low. Seven cards are dealt to each player one at a time in clockwise direction from a well shuffled pack. The balance of the pack is placed in a face-down stock pile in the centre of the table.

The players sort out their hands and play starts with the person on the dealer's left. He places any card face up on the table. The next player adds a card to it which is *either* of the same suit (both Diamonds, Hearts etc.) *or* of the same rank (both 4s, or Aces, or Kings etc.). If a player cannot follow with a card of the same suit or rank, he must pick up a card from the stock pile. Play then passes to the next player on the left.

All 8s are *wild cards*. You can play an 8 at any time (which is especially useful if you are otherwise blocked). The player of the 8 designates what *suit* he wishes the next player to follow with by naming it. So he could lead the 8 ♥ and say "Spades". The next player *must* play a Spade or pick up a card if he cannot follow suit.

The first person to get rid of all his cards scores points calculated by totting up values for the remaining cards in all the other hands:

50 points for every 8.
10 points for each King, Queen and Jack.
1 point for each Ace.

The numerical value of other cards (six points for 6 ♥ etc.).

If the stock pile is used up before anyone "goes out", the game is halted. The winner in this instance is the player with the *lowest* scoring cards in his hand. Points are awarded by subtracting his tally from the total scores of the other hands. The balance becomes his score for that round.

Fish

I strongly recommend that you give this game a try. It is a warm, happy type of game that your whole family will enjoy. To "fish", in this context, means to enquire, to dig for information. Although luck is needed, there is scope for some skill too! If you enjoy "fishing", you will enjoy this game. It is suitable for two to five players.

Requirements: A normal pack of 52 cards.

HOW TO PLAY

The aim of the game is to get rid of all your cards.

The dealer is chosen by cutting the pack. Aces count high and the highest cut wins the dealership. Two or three players receive seven cards each. If there are four or five players they get five cards each. After the deal, the balance of the pack is placed face down in the centre of the table. This is the "Fish" pile.

Each player sorts his cards into groups of the same rank (all the Aces together, all the 7s together, etc.). Care should be taken not accidentally to flash the faces of your cards to your opponents. If *they* give *you* an accidental flash of their cards – *that's different!* Never look a gift horse in the mouth!

The player on the dealer's left starts. Let's call her Suzy. She asks one of the other players (any one) for cards that match one that she already holds, For example, she may hold an 8. She might say "David, give me your eights." If David has any 8s in his hand, he must hand them to her. The same player can then ask either David or one of the other players for other cards, as long as she holds one of the designated rank in her own hand.

Note: You are not allowed to ask for a card unless you hold at least one of similar value in your hand. To do otherwise would be cheating and would ruin the game.

She goes on asking until she draws a blank and asks for a card from someone who cannot supply it. This player tells Suzy to *fish!* She has to pick up a card from the Fish pile.

The player who told her to fish now has the lead and he starts asking the other players for cards. When you have a set of "four of a kind" you place them face up on the table in front of you. The first person to get rid of all their cards, apart from the melds in front of them, wins the game. If two players go out at the same time, the winner is the player with the most melded groups.

WINNING STRATEGY

You must keep your wits about you when playing Fish and a good memory will prove very useful! See if you can work out what sets the other players are collecting. Remember that if you have to fish and pick up a card from the stock pile, *nobody but you knows what it is!* It may be a card that you have previously been asking for and you may now be in a position to meld on your next turn. It may be a card that one of your opponents has previously been asking for. If it is, you can ask him to give you those cards of the same rank when your turn comes around again, and perhaps pick up a complete set in one go!

Pope Joan

While browsing in an antique shop recently, I picked up a circular wooden dish, the interior of which was divided into eight segments. At first I thought that it was for serving antipasto. Then I noticed the inlaid inscriptions that decorated each segment and realised that I had found a beautiful board for playing the traditional British card game, Pope Joan.

Requirements: A pack of **51** cards. The 8 ♦ is removed. About 50 counters for each player. A Pope Joan board. If you possess an *hors d'oeuvre* tray with eight sections you could use that. Eight saucers or small bowls could be used. Failing this, just draw a circle on a piece of card. Divide it into eight sections and label them as shown. Each section should be large enough to hold at least 20 counters.

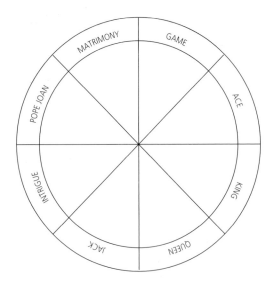

HOW TO PLAY

Three to six players can play. The object of the game is to win as many counters as possible during the course of play.

Pope Joan is the name given to the 9 ♦

A dealer is chosen by cutting. Aces are low. The deal will pass clockwise until everyone has had a deal. Once the dealer has been chosen, the betting begins. Counters are laid on the board. I will describe my preferred method of doing this, although there are other ways (aren't there always?)

Each player (including the dealer) puts four counters in the Pope Joan section; two counters in Matrimony; two counters in Intrigue and one counter in *each* of the other sections.

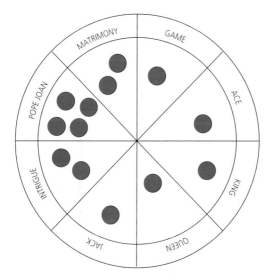

The dealer thoroughly shuffles the pack – has it cut – then deals one card at a time to each player in a clockwise direction, *plus* dealing in an extra hand just before he deals a card to himself. This extra hand is not used or looked at. All players must have an equal number of cards, so any spare cards are put unseen into the extra hand. The top card of the extra hand is turned over to indicate the *trump* suit.

If this card is Pope Joan (9♦), the dealer wins all the counters in the Pope Joan and Game sections of the board. In this event, the deal now passes to the next player on the left and the next round is started. However, the odds are 50-1 against turning up Pope Joan at the start, so it's fairly unlikely. If, instead of Pope Joan, this card is an Ace, King, Queen or a Jack of the trump suit, the dealer claims the chips that are in the appropriately labelled section.

Play begins with the person on the dealer's left. He plays *any* one card face up in the centre of the table and calls out its name, e.g. "5 of Clubs". The player who is holding the 6♣ now plays and calls it, then the holders of the 7♣, 8♣, 9♣ etc. If you are holding several cards that are in sequence you may play them all, calling them as you do so. Play continues until a suit becomes blocked and can proceed no further. There are three reasons for this happening:

- The sequence reaches the blocking King.
- The sequence is in Diamonds and the next card needed would be the 8♦ (removed).
- The card needed is in the extra hand.

When a sequence is *blocked,* the cards dealt thus far are turned face downwards and the player of the last card in the sequence leads off with another card to start a new sequence. This can be in the same suit or in a different suit at the discretion of the player.

As play progresses the players can claim the counters from the sections of the board by playing the following cards:

- The Ace, King, Queen or Jack of the **trump** suit takes all the counters from the appropriate section.
- If the same player lays the Jack and Queen of Trumps in sequence he claims all the counters on Intrigue *plus* the counters on Jack and Queen!

- If the Queen and King of trumps are played in sequence by the same person, he claims all the counters in Matrimony *plus* the counters in King and Queen!

- The player of the 9♦ wins all the counters in the Pope Joan section.
- The first person to play all his cards wins all the counters in the Game section. The other players must also pay him one counter for each card that still remains in their hands *even* if they are the Ace, King, Queen of Jack of Trumps! However, if a player is caught with Pope Joan still unplayed at this stage of the game, he is exempt from this charge.

Unclaimed counters are left on the board and all the players now put in counters for the next round as before. If there are any unclaimed counters left after every player has had a turn as dealer, one further round is played with all cards being dealt face up and without the extra hand. Diamonds automatically become trumps and the counters are claimed by the person receiving the appropriate cards as they appear. The Intrigue and Matrimony counters are divided between the holders of the Jack and Queen, and the Queen and King of Diamonds.

The overall winner of the game is the person who has won the most counters at the end of an agreed period of play.

Klondike

This is the oldest form of "Solitaire" that we know. The rules are very simple. A certain amount of skill is required to play the game well, but however skilful you are, the chances of your completing Klondike successfully are slim!

Requirements: A regular pack of cards, excluding the Jokers.

HOW TO PLAY

Thoroughly shuffle the pack and then deal seven cards in front of you in a row from left to right. The first card is dealt *face up* – the other six *face down*. For clarity of explanation, in the illustration we will number them 1 – 7 from left to right.

A row of six cards is now dealt beneath and overlapping this first row. The first card is dealt *face up* on top of the single face-down card in column 2. The next five cards are dealt *face downwards* on columns 3,4,5,6, and 7 respectively. Next you deal a row of five cards putting the first face-up card on column 3, then a row of four, a row of three, a row of two, and finally a single card *face up* at the base of column 7. Your assembled Klondike tableau will look like this:

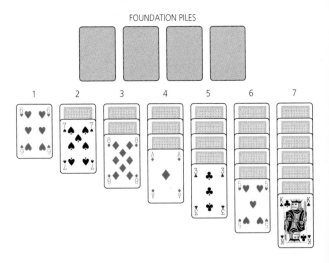

The object of the game is to end up with all the suits arranged in four separate piles stacked in ascending order from Ace (low) to King (high). These are called the *foundation piles* and they are placed above the main tableau as shown in the illustration. As soon as the Ace appears, it should be placed above the tableau to form the starter card of a foundation pile.

So, if there is already an Ace showing in the tableau, remove it and place it in the foundation position. The card that was beneath it is now turned face up. In our illustration the A♦ in column 4, can immediately be transferred up to start a foundation pile, and the card beneath it is then turned face up.

The tableau is now built downwards by placing cards on one another in *descending* order of value and *alternating colours*. In our example again, the black 7 ♠ can be placed on the red 8 ♦, then the red 6 ♥ can be played onto the black 7 ♠. When a blank column appears (as in column 1, after the 6 ♥ was moved), the resulting space can only be occupied by a King. So the K ♣ in column 7 can now be moved to start a new column 1. No more than seven columns are allowed in the tableau.

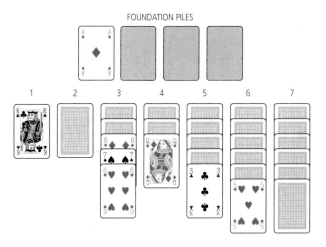

FOUNDATION PILES

Any face-down cards that have now been revealed are turned face up and, if possible, moved onto a downward column of cards or upwards onto a foundation pile. All the face-up cards in a column can be moved onto a different column providing that the bottom face-up card of that column is legally playable.

The balance of the pack that is not used in making the tableau forms a *stock pile*. When you are blocked and no further move is possible, you deal three cards at a time from the stock pile turning them over to expose the third card. The exposed face-up card is now in play, and may be moved onto a down line or directly onto a foundation pile if possible. Then the next face-up card beneath it may also be played if you can. When you become blocked, you deal a further three cards from the stock pile and try to play the exposed third card as before. When you get to the end of the stock pile, all the remaining cards in it are turned face down and groups of three again turned over in search of playable cards.

You do not *have* to move cards directly up to the foundation piles if you think that an alternative move may free some of the trapped face-down cards in the tableau. This is the only skilful part of playing Klondike and your only way of manipulating the 30-1 odds against your successfully completing the game!

You win the game when all four foundation card piles are complete – each one containing all thirteen cards of a suit arranged in order from Ace to King.

Here is a typical game in progress:

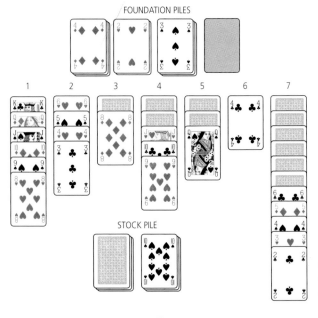

Racing Demon

Any number of players can play this simple, noisy and tremendously exciting family card game. It is based on the game of Klondike which we have just learned to play.

Requirements: A complete pack of cards (minus the Jokers) for each player. Save all your old dog-eared packs especially for this game. Packs with different backs are preferable so that sorting them out at the end becomes easier.

HOW TO PLAY

As a lot of space is required, it is probably best if everybody sits on the floor in a circle facing one another.

Each player shuffles their own pack and forms a Klondike tableau (see page 46). When everyone is ready someone shouts "Go". Each player then starts to play Klondike *as fast as possible*.

Everyone's foundation piles are common ground so, if you cannot lay one of your cards off on your own foundation piles, but can see an opening on one of your opponents' foundation piles, go for it!

The winner is the first person to get rid of all their cards. They must shout "Out". If the game becomes deadlocked, the winner is the person with the highest number of cards in their foundation piles.

Clock Patience

No skill is required to play this version of Patience. The odds of you completing a successful game of Clock Patience are very small. Nevertheless it is great fun to play and is extremely fast moving. It gets its name from the table layout of the cards.

Requirements: A standard pack of 52 cards.

HOW TO PLAY

Shuffle the pack thoroughly and then proceed to deal the first 12 cards face downwards in the style of a clock. The first card is dealt at the one o'clock position, the second at the two o'clock position, and so on until the twelfth card is dealt at the twelve o'clock position.

Deal the thirteenth card face downwards into the centre of the clock circle. The fourteenth card goes at the one o'clock position again, and you continue dealing clockwise around the circle three more times. The 52nd card will end up in the centre of the circle and should be dealt face up.

Say, for example, this last card was the 3♣. You pick it up and slide it face upwards beneath the four face-down cards in the three o'clock position and then turn the top card of this pile face upwards. If it was, for example, the 6♦ you slide it face up beneath the cards in the six o'clock position.

Turn the top card of this pile face upwards and place it face up beneath the position that its value indicates.

If you were to turn up the 6♥ at the six o'clock position, you would still have to put it face up on the bottom of the same pile and turn the next top card over.

Aces = One o'clock
Jacks = Eleven o'clock
Queens = Twelve o'clock
Kings = 13th card and go in the centre pile.

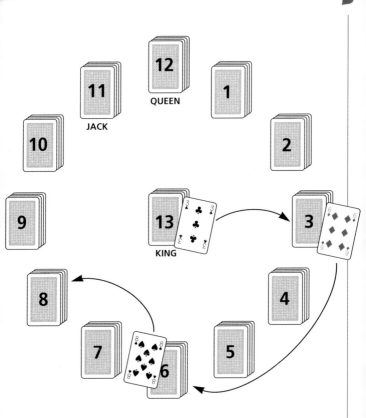

The object of the game is to assemble all the groups of four face-up cards in their appropriate clock positions before the four Kings are turned over.

The Kings will almost certainly be your downfall! All the other sets of four must be grouped before the final King is turned up. As the chances of this happening are quite slim, one extra little rule applies:

Should you turn up the fourth King prematurely, you are allowed to exchange it for any unknown card still face down in the clock spread. Only one exchange of Kings is permitted.

If the King again turns up before the end of the game – tough cookie!

Dreaded Sevens

This is a neat Patience game that was first shown to me when I was in South Africa. I have whiled away many an hour in hotel rooms and airport lounges trying to get it out!

Requirements: All the cards of value 7 and higher, including the four Aces, from a standard pack. Discard the rest.

HOW TO PLAY

Shuffle the 32 cards thoroughly and then deal them *face downwards* into four rows of seven cards. The last four cards form a stock pile which you keep hold of.

The object of the game is to form the cards into this pattern:

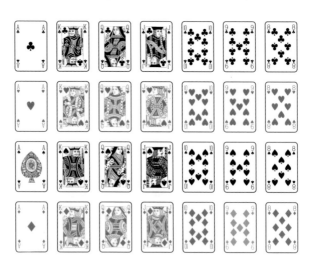

You will notice that the "dreaded" sevens do not figure in the pattern. There is a reason for that, as you will soon discover.

Start by turning any card in the spread face up. In the example illustrated (right), I turned over the card in the position marked by the cross (third card from the right in the second row). It was the K ♠. The

K ♠ is accordingly placed in this designated position and the card that was occupying that space is turned over. It is the 10 ♦. The 10 ♦ is duly put in its correct position and the 9 ♣ that was occupying that space is revealed. That is correctly positioned and the A ♥ that is in this position is moved to its proper place. So the game continues. But there is a snag!

When a dreaded seven is turned up, it is placed at the end of its suit line and a card taken from the stock pile in order to let play continue. A stock pile card is also taken if the space in which you are about to lay a card is empty (as the 10 ♥ position is in my example). The object of the game is to complete the winning tableau before all the dreaded sevens surface.

If you use up the four cards in the stock pile before all your tableau cards are turned face up – turn them over anyway. By some fluke of fortune, they could be in their correct positions! Possible but very unlikely!

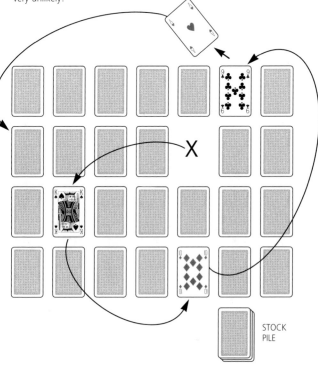

STOCK PILE

Alaska

This is a very satisfying variation of Klondike (see pages 46-48). The layout of the cards results in many more options being available to you, and consequently your strategy can do much to increase your chances of a successful conclusion.

Requirements: A regular 52-card deck.

HOW TO PLAY

Deal the first 28 cards of a thoroughly shuffled pack into the normal Klondike tableau. The remaining 24 cards are dealt *face up* onto columns 2-6. Four cards go on each line. Overlap them so that you can identify all the face-up cards. There is no stock pile. This is how a typical layout should look:

FOUNDATION PILES

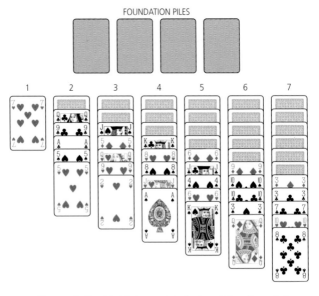

Once again the object is to complete the foundation piles sorted into the relevant suits, starting with the Aces and finishing with the Kings.

A card can only be moved up to the foundation piles when it arrives as the top face-up card of one of the seven columns. If an Ace appears in this position, it *must* be moved up to a foundation pile immediately. When any card other than an Ace becomes available to be moved up, you may exercise discretion – move it up if you wish, or retain it in position for strategical reasons, just as in Klondike. Only Kings can be moved into vacant columns. The exciting difference with Alaska is that any face-up card is available to be played and may be moved with any cards that happen to be above it as a block. The illustration below shows our typical layout after three moves have been made.

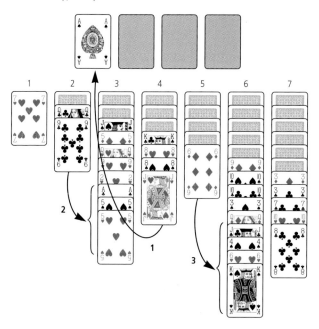

1 The A♠ in column 4 is moved up to the foundation pile.
2 The black A♣ in column 2 is moved (with the two cards above it) and played onto the red 2♥ in column 3.
3 The black J♣ in column 5 is played onto the red Q♦ in column 6. The three cards on top of the J♣ go too.

Can you see any more moves yet? What about 8♥ to 9♣; then Q♦ to K♣; 5♠ to 6♦; A♣ to foundation pile etc, etc. There are plenty of options available, but getting all the cards "out" is harder than it looks.

Pyramid

Like most games of Patience, Pyramid looks easy – but it isn't! You will need a great deal of luck to pull it off successfully.

Requirements: A standard pack of 52 cards.

HOW TO PLAY

Make the following pyramid shape, starting at the top and overlapping the cards as you extend the rows by one card at each level. The pyramid is seven layers deep. The line of seven cards on the bottom level are the only available cards in play at the beginning of the game because they are not covered by overlapping cards.

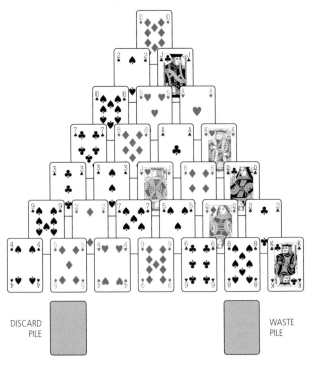

DISCARD
PILE

WASTE
PILE

The object of the game is to form pairs of cards that total 13, and in so doing to eliminate all the 52 cards, i.e. all the pyramid cards and all the cards in the stock pile. For instance, 9 + 4; 6 + 7; Ace + Queen; 2 + Jack; etc. All cards are taken at their face value: Aces = 1; Jacks = 11; Queens = 12; Kings = 13. As Kings = 13 they are played alone. Unlike most Patience games, the suits are ignored in Pyramid.

TYPICAL PAIRS

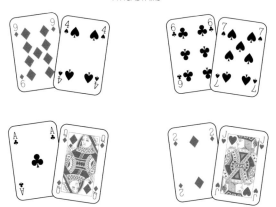

You may be able to find a 13-pair from two cards already in the base line. If this is the case, lift them and place them to one side in a waste pile. The balance of the cards undealt are held in your hand. The top card of this stock pile is turned and you may pair it (make 13) with any card from the bottom row. As you proceed, a pyramid card can only become available if it is *completely free from both cards* that have previously overlapped it. Pairs are taken up and and put to one side in the waste pile. If a stock card cannot be paired, it is placed face up in a separate discard pile.

The next card from the stock is turned and this may either be paired with one of the available cards from the pyramid or with the face-up card from the discard pile. If it cannot be paired, it is dropped face up onto the discard pile.

If the stock pile is exhausted before you have linked up all the pairs, you may pick up the discard pile, turn it face down, and use it as a new stock pile. However, this is only allowed once.

Good luck!

Spider

This game has been described as the king of all Patience games. Although he was not a king, it was certainly played and enjoyed by Franklin D. Roosevelt when he was President of the United States of America. It was reputed to have been his favourite form of Patience. I will leave you to judge whether his enthusiasm for it was well justified.

Requirements: Two standard packs of 52 cards each.

HOW TO PLAY

The two packs are thoroughly shuffled together and then a tableau is dealt out as shown in the accompanying illustration. The first three rows of ten cards are dealt face downwards and overlapping. The final row of ten cards are dealt face up. The face-up cards are the cards available for play.

The object is to build on the Kings in descending order down to the Ace *irrespective of colour or suit.* So a Q♥ may be laid on a K♠, K♥, K♦ or K♣ etc. All face-up cards at the foot of the ten columns are available for play. If a face-down card is opened up when the face-up card that covered it is moved, it is turned face up and duly becomes available for play.

Any of the original ten face-up cards may be played upon another providing that the descending sequence is correctly followed. When a card is transferred, any sequence that is on top and attached to it must be transferred too.

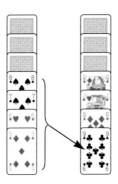

A TYPICAL TRANSFER OF CARDS
BETWEEN COLUMNS

Remember that in Spider suits and colours are not important –
only the numbers.

Aces may not be built upon because they complete the bottom
end of an entire sequence. *Kings may not be lifted until a complete
sequence from King down to Ace has been achieved.* Once this has
been done, the whole sequence is gathered up and put to one side.

When no more moves seem possible the stock pile is picked up
and ten more cards are dealt face up – one on the foot of each column.
All possible moves are now played and then ten further cards are dealt,
and so on. Eventually, after ten rows have been dealt out, only four
cards will remain. These final four cards are dealt onto the first four
(left-hand) columns.

I'm surprised that FDR found the time to play Spider! It is addictive
and at the same time infuriating. You must not jump to obvious
conclusions when you are playing. Although some moves are
straightforward, many times you will be faced with alternative plays. So
the game plants its own minefields which can (and do) explode in your
face. To get this Patience out – *your* patience will be sorely tried!

Have fun!

Carlton

This Solitaire game will keep you on your toes! You will need to give every move careful consideration before making it, because there will often be alternatives open to you to confuse matters. If you like a challenge, you will love Carlton.

Requirements: Two complete packs of cards (excluding Jokers) – 104 cards in all.

HOW TO PLAY

Shuffle the cards thoroughly and then form the tableau illustrated. Start on the left and deal a row of *eight* face-up cards, then a row of *seven*, then *six*, and so on down to the single card on the bottom of the first column. This column should now contain eight cards. These columns of cards are the eight depots.

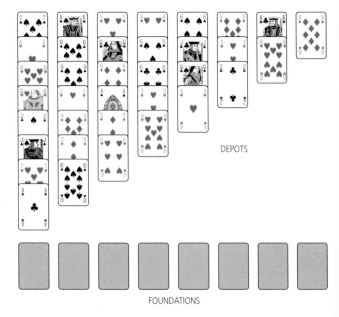

DEPOTS

FOUNDATIONS

The *foundation boxes* are to receive exposed Aces as they are revealed.

You may continue to build with cards in *descending order* and *alternating colours* from the eight vertical depot rows, *and* in *ascending order* and *matching suits* on top of the Aces as they appear and are brought down to the foundation boxes (see illustration below).

When you become blocked and no further moves seem possible, a further row of eight overlapping face-up cards are dealt – one at the end of each of the eight vertical depot lines. Moves are now made, wherever possible, until you get blocked again. Then a further row of eight face-up cards are dealt, and so on.

The object of the game is to end up with all eight completed foundation boxes. Each box will contain all thirteen cards of one suit running from Ace to King.

Only one deal is allowed – so you are not allowed to reshuffle the stock pile if you should get irretrievably stuck!

THIS IS HOW OUR TABLEAU LOOKED AFTER SEVERAL MOVES

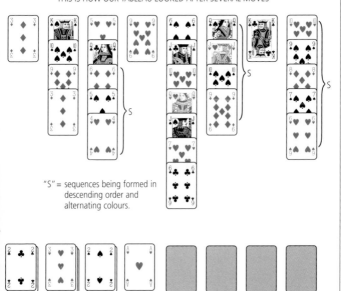

"S" = sequences being formed in descending order and alternating colours.

"F" = Foundation boxes being formed and built upon in matching suits and ascending order.

Monte Carlo

This is another "pairing" Patience game. The object is to get rid of your cards by pairing each one with a card of equal rank. The game is also called Wedding and Double or Quits. It is very easy to play, yet extremely difficult to get out. It's all down to luck "on the day" – just like it is in the casino at Monte Carlo!

Requirements: A standard pack of 52 cards.

HOW TO PLAY
After the pack has been thoroughly shuffled, the top 20 cards are dealt face up into four rows with five cards in each, starting at the top left, i.e. the Q♣ in this example, and working across row-by-row.

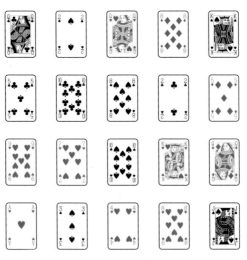

Any two cards of the same rank (number) that adjoin each other – either vertically, horizontally or diagonally – can be removed from the tableau and placed to one side. After each pair is removed, the holes that they have created have to be filled. This is done by shifting the remaining cards along and up, taking care to retain the same order in which they were dealt.

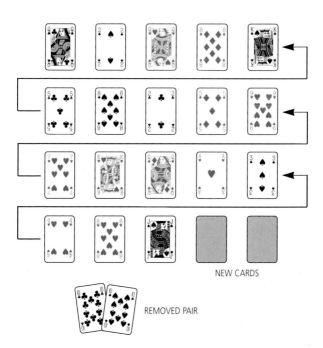

NEW CARDS

REMOVED PAIR

Two spaces will thus be left at the right-hand side of the bottom row. These two spaces are filled by dealing a further two cards face up from the stock pile.

The next pair is removed, the remaining cards shunted round, and two more cards are dealt on the right-hand end of the bottom row. Only one pair may be removed at any one time, because you are only allowed to deal two cards from the stock pile each time.

The "shunting round" of the cards after a pair have been removed will often separate a pair that were previously adjacent to one another. This is half the fun of it, and the reason why you should choose carefully before lifting a pair, if there are several choices open to you.

Play continues in this manner until you reach a total block or (wonder of wonders) go out!

Drop Dead

This fast and furious dice game is perfect for the whole family because any number can play. It is very noisy and fast moving.

Requirements: Five dice.

HOW TO PLAY

The object of the game is to get the highest score at the end of the game.

Each player in turn rolls the five dice. The score is the total of all five dice added together. Now, if that was all there was to it, it would indeed be a rather boring game. However there is a snag...!

If any of the dice show a 2 or a 5, none of the five dice score! The dice bearing the 2 or 5 are removed and you throw the remaining dice, adding up your score as you go.

If the 2s or 5s show again, they are removed.

You will finally be reduced to one die and your play is completed when you throw a 2 or a 5 on this one too. You now **Drop Dead** and the five dice are passed to the next roller.

Scores are recorded and the winner is the person who has the highest score after a pre-arranged number of rounds.

On one occasion, I excelled myself by Dropping Dead on my very first throw! I threw 5, 5, 5, 2, 2! Can you work out the odds against such an unlucky roll happening?

I make it a staggering 3,887-1 chance!

How unlucky can you get?!!!

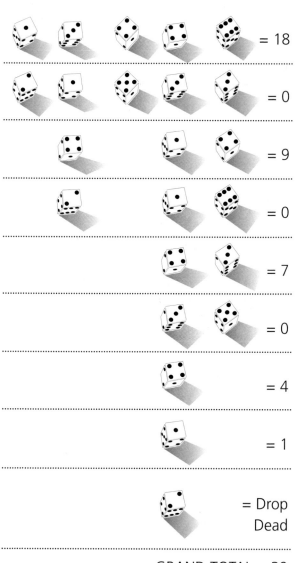

GRAND TOTAL = 39

The Beetle Drive

This is a fast and furious dice game for the whole family. It is very simple to understand, so even quite young children can join in. The more people taking part the better.

Requirements: A die. A dice shaker – a cardboard cup will do fine. A pencil and a sheet of paper for each player. For convenience, I have my sheets marked out like my illustration. A game of Beetle can be played in each of the twelve boxes. If you don't wish to go to the trouble of drawing up the sheet and having photocopies made, blank sheets will do just as well.

HOW TO PLAY

The object of the game is to draw a complete beetle, assembling the component parts of the body by correct rolls of the die. The first drawing will be attempted in Square 1. Subsequent games use subsequently numbered squares.

Each number on the die represents a part of the beetle's anatomy.

- If you roll a 6 you can draw a circle for the *body*.
- A 5 represents the *head*.
- A 4 is the *tail*.
- A 3 is a *leg*.
- A 2 is a *feeler*.
- A 1 represents an *eye*.

Players sit around the table. One person (perhaps the youngest present) starts, shaking the die in the shaker and rolling it out onto the table. He draws what the number on the die represents. The player on his left grabs the shaker and die and has a roll, drawing part of the beetle – if he can. The third person rolls and draws – and so on round and round the circle. The first person to complete a beetle wins the game and shouts out "Beetle" as loudly as possible!

It sounds simple but there are a few pitfalls. Number one: *you must roll a six first to begin*. If you roll a five *before* rolling a six, it does not count because you have not yet got a body to put a head on! Similarly you will have no place for legs or the tail until your beetle's body is drawn. Of course, you cannot draw in eyes and feelers before you have rolled a five for a head.

So, to complete a beetle, you must roll a 6, a 5, a 4, four separate 3s for the legs, two separate 2s for the feelers and two separate 1s for the eyes.

Frustration and excitement build up when you are trying to roll a six to get started and when you keep rolling numbers for parts of the beetle that you have already drawn, when you are trying desperately to roll numbers that you can use.

If six or more people want to play Beetle, you should set up two or more groups – each group with their own die and shaker. This adds an extra dimension to the game because each group competes against the others to complete their beetle first. Play becomes fast and furious because *speed* is vital if someone from your group is going to win.

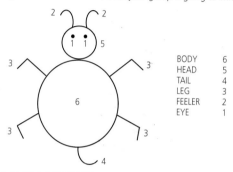

BODY	6
HEAD	5
TAIL	4
LEG	3
FEELER	2
EYE	1

1	2	3	4
5	6	7	8
9	10	11	12

Round the Clock

This simple dice game is suitable for two or more players. It is quick to play and excitement and frustration build in equal measure as you struggle to complete the course.

Requirements: A pair of dice.

HOW TO PLAY

The players take turns to throw both dice. The object of the game is to throw the numbers 1 to 12 in the correct order. The first player to achieve this wins the game.

Scoring: A player is allowed to use the score of a single die or the cumulative total of both. If you roll 1-2 on your first effort, you can immediately try to roll a 3 on your next turn. If you were to throw 1-2 again on this occasion you could total the two dice and count the score as a 3.

Similarly if you are trying to roll a 4 and you roll 4-5, you can immediately try to roll a 6 on your next turn. A roll of 3-1 would also score 4 by adding the two together.

Can you guess how many different rolls are possible with just two dice? Amazingly 36 different rolls are possible when two dice are thrown. To fully understand this, imagine for a moment that you have one red die and one white die. You could roll a 6 on the red die and a 5 on the white die or you could roll a 5 on the red die and 6 on the white one. As you see, two distinctly different rolls. If you total up all the possible combinations, it comes to 36.

The odds are always against you throwing any specific number. The following table should be of interest to you as it shows how many ways there are of rolling any particular number you require with two dice, and the consequent odds against you succeeding. It is nice to know where your money is going!

11 ROLLS 25 – 11 AGAINST
12 ROLLS 2 – 1 AGAINST
13 ROLLS 23 – 13 AGAINST
14 ROLLS 11 – 7 AGAINST
15 ROLLS 7 – 5 AGAINST
16 ROLLS 5 – 4 AGAINST
6 ROLLS 5 – 1 AGAINST
5 ROLLS 31 – 5 AGAINST
4 ROLLS 8 – 1 AGAINST
3 ROLLS 11 – 1 AGAINST
2 ROLLS 17 – 1 AGAINST
1 ROLL 35 – 1 AGAINST

1 2 3 4 5 6 7 8 9 10 11 12

Put and Take

When I was a child I used to play this game regularly with my parents. It is years since I have seen anyone playing it, so I pass it on to you in the hope that together we may start a revival!

Requirements: One die. One marker token (a coin or any other small object will do). Money, counters, matches or whatever you decide to play for. Start with about 25 units each. You will also need to copy the "wheel" design illustrated onto a piece of paper or cardboard. You may be able to photocopy my design from this book, and scale it up to a more convenient size.

HOW TO PLAY:

All players put six units in a pool. The marker token is placed on the "Take All" segment of the "wheel". Each person rolls the die once to determine who will start first. The highest number wins and this player rolls the die again. The token is moved around the wheel in a clockwise direction. The player (sometimes all the players) must act upon the instruction written on the segment on which the token lands.

- If the first player rolled a 1, he would move to "All Put Two". All players must, therefore, put two more units into the pot.
- If he rolls 2, he alone must put one more unit into the pot.
- If he rolls 3, he takes two and removes his winnings from the pot.
- If he rolls 4, all put one more unit into the pot.
- If he rolls 5, he takes one winning unit from the pot.
- If he rolls 6, he puts two extra units in the pot.

The play passes around the table clockwise and the next person begins his turn from where the token now lies. If this player lands on the "extra turn", he gets just that – another roll of the die.

Whoever lands on "take all" hits the jackpot and wins all the units in the pot. When this happens or when the pot is otherwise emptied, a new pot is formed by the donation of six further units from each player.

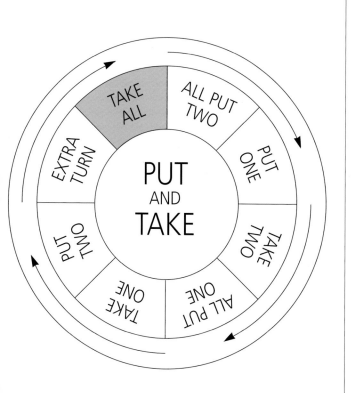

TAKE ALL

ALL PUT TWO

EXTRA TURN

PUT ONE

PUT AND TAKE

PUT TWO

TAKE TWO

TAKE ONE

ALL PUT ONE

Going to Boston

first saw this American game played during my first visit to New York in 1965. I was not "going to Boston" – just visiting friends in Manhattan!

Requirements: Three dice. A shaker. Any number can play although the game is best with three or four participants.

HOW TO PLAY

A stake is first decided upon and each player puts this stake in the pot. The players decide beforehand how many rounds will be played before the result is calculated.

The first player rolls all three dice from the shaker. The highest scoring die is left on the table and the other two are re-thrown from the shaker. If you roll three 6s on the first roll – too bad! Two of the dice must be re-rolled. Of these two, the higher is left and the third re-thrown. If you throw a double, it's again tough luck. One die must be re-rolled. The scores on the three dice are now added together and this is the score for the first player.

The other players now take it in turns to roll the dice. The winner is the roller with the highest score at the end of the predetermined number of rounds. In the event of a tie, a play-off round is played between the top scorers.

EXAMPLE ROLL:

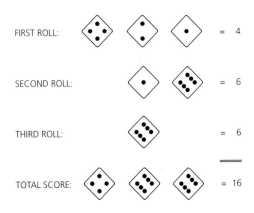

FIRST ROLL:		= 4
SECOND ROLL:		= 6
THIRD ROLL:		= 6
TOTAL SCORE:		= 16

Twenty-One

This is really a variation of the card game called Pontoon or Blackjack (see pages 16-19), except that the players compete against one another rather than the bank!

Requirements: Two dice. Lots of money, counters or matches!

HOW TO PLAY

Each player puts an equal stake into the pot. The object of the game is to score 21 or as near to 21 as possible without "busting" your total. A player may have as many rolls as he wishes in order to complete his turn and get as close to 21 as he dare.

When a total of 14 or more is reached, the player is allowed to use only one die to increase his score. Any person scoring over 21 has "busted" and is out.

The winner is the player who gets closest to 21. In the event of a tie, the pot may be shared or a single die rolled to determine the outright winner.

WINNING STRATEGY

It is always nice to play a game well! Here are a few tips to help you:

- A knowledge of the odds against rolling any given number will be of tremendous help to you in this game. Refer to the list on page 69 to see what these odds are.
- If your score is 17 or under, it is worth having one further roll with the single die.
- Going last is very advantageous because you will then know the score to beat or equal. For example, if you have reached 18 or 19 and someone else has already scored 20 or 21, it would be folly not to try for the 2 or 3 that you require to reach 21. You can't win as you stand, so you may as well "go for it"!

Fifty!

I still see this game being played in various parts of the world. It amazes me because, if you know the secret, you can *always win!* It is a game for two players.

Requirements: Two dice (one for each player).

HOW TO PLAY

You show a number on your die – your opponent shows a number too. The numbers are added together. You then show another number and so does your opponent. The total of these two dice are added to the total of the first two. Play proceeds like this. The first player to reach *exactly* 50 wins the game!

WINNING STRATEGY

The *key numbers* to remember are **1 – 8 – 15 – 22 – 29 – 36** and **43.** Each number is an increase of 7 on its predecessor so you should have little trouble in committing this list to memory. When you have done that, you will never lose a game of fifty!

Your secret is to latch on to a "Key Number" as quickly as you can – then hop from one key number to the next until you reach 43. Whatever your opponent now plays you must be able to reach 50 on your next turn!

If you start, always begin with ⚀.

Whatever your opponent now plays, you must be able to reach 8 on your next go.

Then, whatever your opponent plays after you have reached 8, just go to your next key number – **you can't lose!**

- If he starts with ⚅, you play ⚁
- If he starts with ⚄, you play ⚂
- If he starts with ⚃, you play ⚃
- If he starts with ⚂, you play ⚄
- If he starts with ⚁, you play ⚅

If he starts with ⚀, you play ⚀, then keep playing until you are able to reach one of the key numbers – which shouldn't be too difficult, unless your opponent knows the secret too!

Double Fifty

This is a very fast moving dice game that is suitable for any number of players. Once you have learned how to play Fifty, you will find this an enjoyable variation on the theme.

Requirements: A pair of dice. Paper and pencil for scoring.

HOW TO PLAY

Each player rolls both dice. You score only when you roll doubles – two 1s, two 2s, two 3s, etc. The winner is the first person to reach a score of fifty.

The scoring is as follows:
- Double one ⚀ ⚀ scores 5 points.
- Double two ⚁ ⚁ scores 5 points.
- Double four ⚃ ⚃ scores 5 points.
- Double five ⚄ ⚄ scores 5 points.
- Double six ⚅ ⚅ scores 25 points.

Beware! If you are unlucky enough to roll double three ⚂ ⚂, you must cancel out your existing score and start again at zero!

WHAT ARE THE ODDS?

The odds against throwing any double are 30-6 or 5-1 against. The odds against throwing a *specific* double, such as ⚂ ⚂, are 35-1 against. So you can count yourself unlucky if the dreaded double three appears as one of your rolls.

75

One to Eighteen

This is a very frustrating game. Frustrating – yet very exciting! Any number can play, although it is best enjoyed with a group of three or four.

Requirements: Three dice.

HOW TO PLAY

The players roll the dice alternately. The object is to roll the numbers from 1 to 18 *in sequence* before your opponents. All three dice are rolled each time.

Scoring allows you to count the face value of an individual die, and the total value of combinations of dice added together.

So if a ⚀ appears among the three, you are allowed to disregard the other two dice and score 1.

If you are attempting to score 2 and a ⚁ appears, you can score 2.

You are also allowed to score 2 in this next example because you are allowed to total two or more dice to achieve your desired total: ⚀ ⚀ ⚄

If you are lucky enough to roll ⚀ ⚁ ⚂ with your first roll, you score all three face values and can immediately go on to attempt to score a 4 on your next roll!

You are only allowed to use the value of a die *once* in each cast. So, if you were aiming to score 4 and you rolled: ⚁ ⚁ ⚂ , you would not be allowed to score 5 as well by adding a two and the three together, because you have already used both 2s to get your score of 4.

Crag

This is, in my opinion, the best dice game. I hope that you will agree.
Two or more people can play, but with more than four players it
tends to drag a bit, so try to keep playing groups relatively small.

Requirements: Three dice. A pencil and score card made out as the
example illustrated. This will take you a while to prepare but is essential
for accurate scoring.

	PLAYER 1	PLAYER 2	PLAYER 3	PLAYER 4
ONES				
TWOS				
THREES				
FOURS				
FIVES				
SIXES				
ODD STRAIGHT (20 pts)				
EVEN STRAIGHT (20 pts)				
LOW STRAIGHT (20 pts)				
HIGH STRAIGHT (20 pts)				
THREE OF A KIND (25 pts)				
THIRTEEN (30 pts)				
CRAG (50 pts)				
TOTAL				

HOW TO PLAY

Each player must try to make the highest score possible by aiming to achieve the dice patterns illustrated below. There are a few rules concerning the throw of the dice that you must remember.

- The three dice are thrown together and a player may take a second throw to try to improve the position, rolling one, two or even all three dice, again.
- If a pattern is made after the two throws, the score is entered on the chart in the appropriate position.
- The next player now has his two throws, and so on in rotation.
- Sometimes it is possible to score *more* than one pattern with the same dice. You must decide which one of the combinations to go for and state your preference before your second throw. You are not allowed to change your mind!
- No pattern – no score!
- You are not allowed to claim the same pattern twice. If thrown, this second pattern will not count for a score.
- The winner is the person who achieves all the patterns first or the person who has the highest score when it is time to go to bed!

THE SCORING PATTERNS

Ones: You need at least two and you score 1 point for each. (Maximum 3 points)

Twos: At least two. Score 2 points for each. (Maximum 6 points)

Threes: At least two. Score 3 points for each. (Maximum 9 points)

Fours: At least two. Score 4 points for each. (Maximum 12 points)

Fives: At least two. Score 5 points for each. (Maximum 15 points)

Sixes: At least two. Score 6 points for each. (Maximum 18 points)

Odd Straight: Score 20 points

Even Straight: Score 20 points

Low Straight: Score 20 points.

High Straight: Score 20 points.

Three of a Kind:
All three dice the same.
Score 25 points

Thirteen: Total 13 with *no doubles*. Score 30 points.

Crag: Total 13 *with doubles*. Score 50 points.

WINNING STRATEGY

This is a very skilful game. Luck has a part to play of course, but you can greatly enhance your chances of winning by carefully selecting the dice that you wish to stand and those that you wish to re-throw.

The last seven combinations on the score sheet are the most difficult to throw, therefore it makes good sense to try for these *first*.

Remember that the person who is first to throw all thirteen patterns wins.

Fivestones

This exciting game makes wonderful family fun. I first played it 55 years ago and over the years I have learned many variations. They all require a certain amount of dexterity and hand-eye co-ordination. Most of them are played with only one hand. You can practise these exercises on you own. When played as a competitive game, the object is to see who can successfully complete the most disciplines, without making a mistake.

Requirements: Five dice.

HOW TO PLAY

Attempt each feat in sequence. You must successfully achieve each challenge before you are allowed to progress to the next one. This game is best played on a carpeted floor or, even better, a sandy beach on an exotic tropical island!

Ones Put four dice on the ground. Hold one die in your hand. Throw this die into the air, with the same hand pick up one of the dice from the floor and try to catch the die that you have thrown into the air before it drops on the floor. Keep these two dice in your hand and throw one of them into the air. Pick up another die from the floor and catch the descending die before it drops to the floor. Carry on until you have picked up and caught all the dice and are holding them in one hand.

Twos Put the dice on the floor. Pick up one die with your right hand. Throw it into the air and pick up *two* dice from the floor – then catch the descending die before it touches the ground. Throw one of the dice that you are holding into the air and pick up the remaining two dice from the floor. You can use "throws and catches" to brush the dice closer together (using the side of your hand) so that they are easier to pick up. Now you can try...

Threes This is similar to twos, only first you must pick up three dice from the floor and then the last single one. Now go on to...

Fours Scatter the dice on the floor. Pick up one, throw it up and, while it is in mid-air, pick up the other four dice in one swoop! Now things get more difficult...

Crabs Throw one die into the air and catch it on the *back* of your hand. While balancing it there, you must manoeuvre the four remaining dice into the gaps between your fingers and thumb. Squeeze your fingers together to grip the dice and lift them up; at the same time toss the die on the back of you hand into the air. Turn your hand over to catch the descending die and at the same time wiggle your fingers and thumb to settle the other four safely into your palm... If that seems hard, wait until you try this one...

Topsy-turvy All five dice are on the floor. Pick up one, throw it into the air and catch it on the back of your hand. Throw it into the air from the back of your hand, pick up a die from the floor and catch the descending die. Throw both dice into the air and catch them on the back of your hand. Toss them up in the air from the back of your hand and pick up another die, then catch the two descending dice. Throw the three dice into the air and catch them on the back of your hand. Toss them up again and pick up another die, then catch the three airborne dice before they hit the floor. Throw the four dice into the air and catch them on the back of your hand. Toss them up again, picking up the last die and catch the four descending dice. Now try this...

Five A Side Hold all five dice in your right hand. Throw them into the air and try to catch them all on the back of your hand! Now toss them in the air from the back of your hand and catch them in the palm of your hand again. If you can do that, you have certainly mastered Fivestones!

Golf

Golf players are usually fanatics about their sport, so it should come as no surprise that there is a dice game that imitates their favourite pastime.

Requirements: Three dice. A pencil and paper for scoring. Make your chart out like this:

HOLE	PLAYER 1	PLAYER 2	PLAYER 3	PLAYER 4
1				
2				
3				
4				
5				
6				
7				
8				
9				
10				
11				
12				
13				
14				
15				
16				
17				
18				
TOTALS				

HOW TO PLAY

The playing order is determined by each player rolling a die. The highest score "tees off". A player keeps rolling all three dice together until a double is rolled. When you roll a double, you are "in the hole". The number of rolls taken signifies the number of strokes taken on this hole and this number is entered on the chart.

The next player now rolls until he gets a double and his score is entered under his column. Play continues in this way.

If you roll a triple (all three dice the same) it counts as a *birdie* and your overall score for the hole is reduced by one stroke. If they are all sixes, it's an *eagle,* and two strokes may be deducted from your score. They are about as elusive as they are in the real game!

You can play Golf over the short course of nine holes or the complete long course of eighteen holes. The winner is naturally the golfer with the *lowest* score. He should buy everyone a drink in the nineteenth hole!

Potty

This game is best played with real money. Matches, counters or buttons will do, but nothing beats the excitement of playing with coins – even low denomination ones! Potty is best played with *at least* four people.

Requirements: Two dice. Three coins for each player. A pot, cup or saucer.

HOW TO PLAY

A player throws both dice just once before passing them to the player on his left. If his throw does *not* show a ⚀ or a ⚅, no action is taken and the second player now rolls the dice.

- If, however, one of the dice shows a ⚀, the player has to put *one* coin in the pot.

- If he rolls ⚀ ⚀, he must put *two* coins in the pot.

- If he rolls a ⚅, he must give *one* of his coins to the person on his left.

- If he rolls ⚅ ⚅, he must give *two* coins to the person on his left.

When you have no more coins left you miss your turn, but you are not out of the game. Yet! You may receive penalty coins from the player on your right and so get back in play again.

When only one coin remains, its owner is given *three* rolls of the dice. If he can do this without throwing a six, he wins all the coins in the pot. If, during these three rolls, he does throw a six, he has to give the coin to the person on his left who now has three rolls and similarly tries *not* to roll a six. Play continues in this fashion until one of the players avoids throwing a six and thus scoops the pot. Potty!

Chicago

Eleven possible scores can be made when two dice are rolled together and this game is based upon that fact. Any number of people can play it, so Chicago is good family entertainment when there are lots of people around.

Requirements: Two dice.

HOW TO PLAY

Eleven rounds are played in all. The players are allowed only one roll of the dice per round.

In the first round all the players try to roll a total of 2. In the second round all the players try to roll a total of 3. The next round they all try for a total of 4; and so on until the eleven rounds have been completed.

If you roll the correct number in the appropriate round you add this score to your personal total. For example, if you succeeded in rolling totals of 2, 6, 9 and 10 when required, your total would be 27. The winner is the highest scorer after all the rounds have been completed.

WHAT ARE THE ODDS

It helps in this game to know just what you are up against in terms of the probability of rolling specific totals. As you will see from this table, the hardest shots are and daunting 35-1 chances. Here is the full picture:

Against rolling a total of   2 = 35-1
Against rolling a total of   3 = 17-1
Against rolling a total of   4 = 11-1
Against rolling a total of   5 = 8-1
Against rolling a total of   6 = 31-5
Against rolling a total of   7 = 5-1
Against rolling a total of   8 = 31-5
Against rolling a total of   9 = 8-1
Against rolling a total of   10 = 11-1
Against rolling a total of   11 = 17-1
Against rolling a total of   12 = 35-1

Centennial

This game is very tricky! Up to eight players can take part. You must keep your wits about you because other players are allowed to "steal" your score if you overlook something. Nasty!

Requirements: Three dice. A distinctive easily recognized token for each player. A pencil and paper. You must prepare a large chart with twelve numbered boxes, each one large enough to hold a few of the tokens should they land upon it. The illustration shows how it should look.

HOW TO PLAY

Each player attempts to move his token up the board from numbers 1 to 12 and then back again. The first one home wins!

A running order is decided in the usual way by rolling a die – highest goes first. To start, the first player must roll a ⚀. To move further, he must then roll a ⚁ then a ⚂, and so on. Having reached 12 he must roll 12 *again,* then 11, 10, 9 etc in descending order to get back to box 1.

A player may use any number of the three dice to reach a required total and numbers rolled may be used *more than once.* For example if a player should roll ⚀ ⚁ ⚂, he can move to box 1 for the ⚀, box 2 for the ⚁, box 3 for the ⚂, box 4 for the ⚀ and the ⚂, box 5 for the ⚁ and the ⚂, and box 6 for the ⚀, the ⚁, and the ⚂. Not bad!

The really sneaky feature of this game is the fact that an opponent can "pinch" a score from you if you have not used it yourself, as long as he can use it straight away, and does so as soon as you pass the dice, signifying the end of your turn. So keep alert at all times and see if you can score off your opponents in this way! It is a bit like being "huffed" at draughts when your opponent can remove one of your pieces from the board if it could have taken his piece but you overlooked the winning move!

	12	
	11	
	10	
	9	
	8	
	7	
	6	
	5	
	4	
	3	
	2	
START	1	FINISH

Pig

This simple game causes great excitement in my family whenever we play it. The element of *choice* comes into play and you have only yourself to blame if you push your luck too far! Any number of people can play.

Requirements: A single die. A pencil and paper for scoring.

HOW TO PLAY
Each player rolls the die once in order to establish a playing order. The *lowest* roller plays first, then the second lowest, and so on. This running order is important because the first and last rollers have an advantage over the other players. A series of games should be played and the order rotated so that each person gets to play from an advantageous position.

The aim of the game is to score 101; the first person to do this wins the game. The first player rolls the die *as many times as he wishes,* totalling these rolls as he does so. The player can stop any time that he wishes, pass the die to the next player and record his score for that round on the paper. The snag is that if he rolls a ⚀, he must stop immediately, lose the score that he has accumulated in that round and pass the die to the next player!

WINNING STRATEGY
It is possible to run up quite a large score before rolling a ⚀. 50 or more can often be achieved. However, you should be content with rolls of around 15 unless you are chasing someone else's higher total. Of course, if you are a long way behind and one of the other player's total is fast approaching the 101 target, you should go for it and try to beat the odds. You have (almost) lost anyway so what have you go to lose? You may just pull it off! Remember that the odds of you rolling a ⚀ are 5-1 against, so all things being equal, you should have a run of successful throws before a ⚀ shows up.

VARIATION

I call this variation Fat Pig! For this you need two dice and a score sheet. Play is the same as in Pig except that two dice are rolled, rather than one.

A ⚀ on either dice immediately cancels out your score for that turn and the dice are passed on. A roll of ⚀ ⚀, however, gains you a bonus of 25 points and you continue rolling if you choose to.

All other doubles count *double* for your score, so...

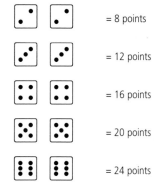

= 8 points

= 12 points

= 16 points

= 20 points

= 24 points

The object of the game is the same – to get to 101 before anyone else does.

Shut the Box

We have a very attractive piece of apparatus at home to play Shut the Box. I have included the game in this book because, nice as it is to have a purpose-made wooden set, it can just as easily be played with two dice and a pencil and paper.

Requirements: Two dice. Nine coins, counters or draughts pieces. A pencil and paper.

HOW TO PLAY

Draw nine square boxes in a row. Make them large enough to contain the coin or markers that you have chosen to use. Number the boxes boldly from 1 to 9.

The object of the game is to cover as many boxes as possible with the counters, using the values of the dice you roll to determine which numbers you can cross off. An order of play is first established by each player rolling the dice once. The highest scorer starts.

He then rolls the two dice and *must use the full score of this roll* to block out certain numbers from the row.

Say he rolled 🎲 🎲, he could place:

- a single counter on the 8 box,
- or one on the 3 and another on the 5 box,
- or one on the 1 and another on the 7 box,
- or one on the 6 and another on the 2 box,
- or one on the 1, another on the 2 and a third on the 5 box,
- or cover the 1, 3, and 4 boxes.

You split up your total as you think best to eliminate a number or combination of numbers from those available.

After making his move, the player rolls again and continues to cover up available boxes. Once boxes 7, 8 and 9 are all covered, a player is allowed to continue rolling with just one die. Once a number has been covered, it is no longer available. It cannot be used twice. His play continues until he throws an unusable total. He now totals up the numbers of the uncovered boxes and this total is scored against him.

Play now passes to the next person. The winner is the person with the *lowest* score after a predetermined number of rounds.

This game originated in Northern France about 200 years ago. If you like it, you may decide to purchase a commercial version to keep in the games cupboard. These are widely available and consist of a wooden box with nine numbered compartments that may be covered with sliding shutters and a baize-lined tray section in which to roll the dice.

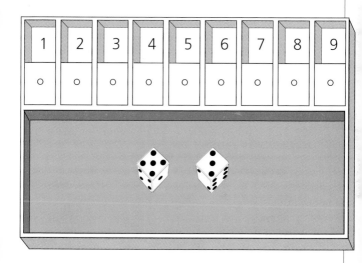

Helping Hands

I first saw this game being played only a few months ago in Italy. After further research I was amazed to discover that this is one of the oldest dice games known to man. It is fun to play and suitable for the whole family. Although any number can play, it is at its very best when played by six people.

Requirements: Two dice. Ten counters for each player.

HOW TO PLAY

The object is to get rid of all your counters. Each player is given ten counters and then allocated a number from 1 to 6. If there are only two players, one of them represents 1, 2 and 3 while the other represents 4, 5 and 6. With three players they get two numbers each: 1 and 2, 3 and 4, 5 and 6 respectively. Four players get one number each and the numbers 5 and 6 are ignored. WIth 5 players you ignore the number 6 and allocate numbers from 1 to 5 to the players.

A playing order is obtained in the usual way by rolling a die – highest goes first. The first to play rolls the dice. According to whatever numbers show, the persons representing those numbers must discard one counter into the middle of the table. So, if the roll was ⚅ ⚀, player number 6 and player number 1 each get rid of one of their counters. If ⚄ ⚄ was rolled, then that player gets rid of *two* counters!

The game is deceptively simple and yet can generate tremendous excitement. It is a great favourite with young children as they compete on equal terms with the grown-ups, and love it when they come out on top.

Yankee Grab

As you would suspect from the title, this game has its origins in the United States. I have seen it played by youths on street corners in Manhattan for horrendous sums of money! My family literally play it for peanuts!

Requirements: Three dice. As many players as you can muster.

HOW TO PLAY

Set a running order in the usual way and then take turns to roll all three dice together. The object of the game is to score the highest number possible – as near to the maximum 18 as you can. Each player is allowed no more than three rolls per round.

By way of explanation, the first player rolls the dice. The highest scoring die is left standing and the other two dice may be re-thrown in an effort to improve them. The lowest scoring of these two may then be re-thrown. (This is, of course, optional – if you want to "stick" after your first roll, you can). Obviously if you rolled ⚅ ⚅ ⚅ on your first roll, you wouldn't need your second and third rolls, would you?

The player now records the final total of his rolls.

The next player now rolls the dice. When everyone has rolled, the round is complete and the person with the highest score wins. This is quite a quick game so it is best to play five or ten rounds and find a supreme champion!

Indian Dice

This is a very strange title for a game that appears to have been invented in America! It was originally used as a substitute for the card game Poker and shares many of the rules of this game. Unlike Poker, however, it is a game of pure luck – skill is not necessary for success, although some tactical decisions have to be made.

Requirements: Five dice.

HOW TO PLAY

Each player contributes a unit to the pot. The object of the game is to roll the dice no more than three times in an attempt to get the best "hand" (combination of dice) possible. The best hand at the end of the round scoops the pot! To make things interesting, in Indian Dice all ⚀'s are "wild cards" or "Jokers" and may represent any number that you wish. A playing order is arrived at by rolling a die each. The highest goes first.

If a player throws a reasonable pattern with his *first* throw, he may well decide not to take advantage of his other two throws and "stand". This is extremely good strategy because the players that follow are not allowed to use more throws than the first player has taken. Similarly, if after two rolls he wishes to stand, he may also do so.

The onus is then on the other rollers to do better with the same number or even fewer rolls. Remember that 6 is high, 2 is low. The accompanying illustration shows the ranking system for scoring hands.

WINNING STRATEGY
- If your first roll is reasonably good, you would be well advised to let it stand, thus forcing your opponents to beat you in one roll.
- Never re-roll ⚀'s

The following list shows all the possible hands in *descending* order of strength. In the event of tied hands, pure scores that do *not* include Jokers win. If hands are still tied – for example, two players have both thrown a natural full house, the hand with the higher-ranking values wins. If hands are exactly tied (i.e. you have both thrown three 4s), both players throw a single die to decide the outright winner – the highest score wins.

WINNING HANDS

Five of a kind:  etc

A run: etc

Four of a kind: etc

Full house:
(three of a kind
plus any pair)   etc

Three of a kind: etc

Two pairs: etc

One pair: etc

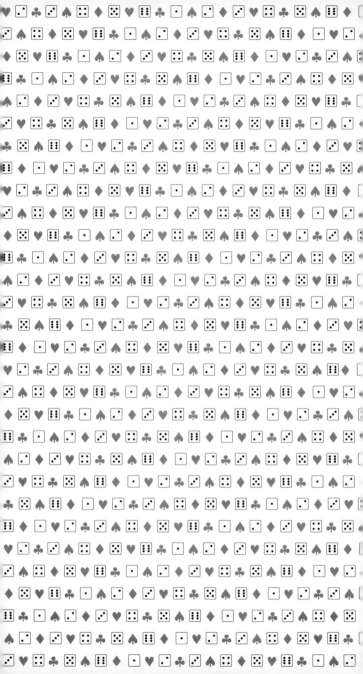